BY THE EDITORS OF

CONSUMER GUIDE®

SIMPSON MANIA

THE HISTORY OF TV'S FIRST FAMILY

PROFILES • CLOTHING • REVIEWS • MERCHANDISE • TRIVIA • ETC.

Steve Dale
Shane Tritsch

Publications International, Ltd.

Steve Dale writes features and the "Celebrity Watch" column for the *Chicago Tribune*. He also covers entertainment in the Chicago area for *People* magazine, as well as writing an entertainment column for *Inside Chicago*. In the past, Mr. Dale has served as entertainment critic for several Chicago area radio stations.

Shane Tritsch is a graduate of the Medill School of Journalism at Northwestern University. He is currently associate editor at *Inside Chicago*. Mr. Tritsch also writes film reviews on a free-lance basis for many publications.

PICTURE CREDITS:
ABC-TV: 21(bottom); **Sam Griffith Photography:** 30, 31, 32, 34, 35; **Phil Huber/Black Star:** 29, 33; **Alan P. Levenson/Onyx:** 37; **Diana Lyn/Shooting Star:** 41; **Randee St. Nicholas/NBC:** 44(left); **Randi St. Nichols/© Fox Broadcasting Company:** 4(bottom), 43; **Photofest:** 7, 12, 14, 18, 19; **Photofest/© Hanna-Barbera Productions, Inc.:** 6, 20; **Aaron Rapoport/© Fox Broadcasting Company:** 21(top); **Bonnie Schiffman/Onyx:** 8, 9, 38, 39, 40; **Nicholas Secor/Gamma-Liaison:** 45(right); **TM & © Twentieth Century Fox Film Corporation 1990:** 5, 10, 11, 13, 15, 16, 17, 22, 24, 36; **TM & © Twentieth Century Fox Film Corporation 1990/Shooting Star:** 23.

Beach towel made by a la carte/saydah. Water bottle made by Betras Plastics, Inc. Underwear made by Boxer Rebellion. Buttons made by Button-Up Co. Bumper stickers made by N.J. Croce Co. Car window signs made by H & L Enterprises. Notepad made by Legends of Entertainment. Hats made by NOVA. T-shirts made by S.S.I. Bart poster made by Western Graphics Corp.

Publications International, Ltd.

CONTENTS

The Story Behind Making

The Simpsons

Tracey Ullman's TV show was the first showcase for The Simpsons.

"Why you little..." says actor Dan Castellaneta. He looks as annoyed in the flesh as Homer J. Simpson will look on TV after Castellaneta's voice is matched with Homer's animated image.

Standing a few feet away in the same studio is actress Nancy Cartwright, who plays Bart Simpson, Homer's son. "Don't have a cow, Homer," she snaps back.

Some television series are planned out every step of the way. But no one could have guessed the way *The Simpsons* fell into place. And actor Harry Shearer, who plays several extra roles in the program, thinks that's one reason *The Simpsons* has done so well.

"Most programs are test marketed by focus groups [sample viewers]," said Shearer to Steve Dale, a columnist with *Inside Chicago*. "Then the networks listen to everyone; they try so hard to make the characters likable to everyone. There was no time for that with *The Simpsons* because it all happened so quickly."

The Simpson family fit right in with the rest of the crazy cast on The Tracey Ullman Show.

A scene from "There's No Disgrace Like Home," an episode that aired during the first season of The Simpsons. The TV series started as short bits on The Tracey Ullman Show.

"...*The Simpsons* throwaway [casual] lines were better than the best one-liners on most other comedies."

It all started with James L. Brooks, executive producer of *The Tracey Ullman Show*. Brooks wanted to add a crazed cartoon to Ullman's already wacky cast of characters. He found the idea hanging on his office wall—a framed cartoon from a comic strip.

Brooks convinced the cartoon's author, Matt Groening, (his name rhymes with "raining"), to invent some animated snips for the Ullman show. Groening wrote and directed 30- and 60-second bits to lead in to and out of commercials. The bug-eyed Simpson family made fun of parents, teachers, the police, doctors, television, and themselves. And the people watching the Ullman show loved them. "From the start, *The Simpsons* throwaway [casual] lines were better than the best one-liners on most other comedies," said *USA Today* TV critic Matt Roush.

Grabbing the chance, Brooks made the kind of smooth move that would make Bart proud. Quicker than Bart could say, "Aye, caramba!" Brooks pushed for his Gracie Films company to produce a half-hour animated sitcom.

In an unusual reaction, the folks at the Fox network just about had a cow. Unlike the other networks, the Fox network is willing to take risks.

The Simpsons was not the first animated prime-time TV show. Shows like The Flintstones helped pave the way.

The Simpsons almost didn't make it on TV.

It's been 30 years since *The Flintstones*—Fred, Wilma, Barney, and Betty—appeared on prime-time TV. Some 28 years have passed since George Jetson of *The Jetsons* first went to work for Spacely Sprockets. There hasn't been as hot an animated prime-time show since then.

At first, Fox wanted to ease *The Simpsons* into America's living rooms with several "specials." Fox wanted to test-market the oddball family all the way.

But Brooks firmly refused. "Thank goodness," said Shearer. "The characters would have lost their edge, and the show never would have been the same."

The Simpsons isn't the first TV series that almost didn't make it. CBS almost pulled *All in the Family* after the first episode, and NBC thought *Saturday Night Live* was a concept that would never work. Brooks, an experienced TV producer and director, kept pushing for a regular series. Finally, Fox agreed. According to several reports, the network turned from doubter to cheerleader practically overnight.

The *Simpsons* first aired on December 17, 1989. It was a half-hour-long Christmas special called "The Simpsons Roasting on an Open Fire." It wasn't the kind of holiday cheer the network usually presents.

Normally, Charlie Brown tries to find the true meaning of Christmas. But Bart demands to be tattooed, man. Bart sneers, "There's only one fat guy who brings us presents, and his name isn't Santa." In the meantime, the "fat guy," Homer, loses what little Christmas money he has at the dog track. But all ends well with the dog at the Simpson household.

January 14, 1990, marked the beginning of what Groening has called a hallucination of a sitcom. The camera peeks into the Springfield Elementary School. Once again, Bart has to stay after school and write sentences on the blackboard. ("I will not instigate a revolution." "I will not waste chalk.") The bell rings and he bolts on his skateboard. Mom Marge waits in a checkout line while the clerk accidentally passes baby Maggie over the electronic product-code reader. Sister Lisa and her saxophone bike home after band practice. And Homer finishes his shift in a nuclear power plant by accidentally carrying out a bit of radioactive waste. This family is frantic to make it home in time to gather in front of the TV to watch *The Simpsons*.

Everyone is frantic to get home in time to gather in front of the TV to watch *The Simpsons*.

All in the Family dealt with explosive issues and themes, just as The Simpsons does. Both families have a blue-collar background and treat each other in the same rough, but loving, manner.

Matt Groening's comic strip starring Binky the Rabbit was the inspiration for The Simpsons.

As many as 14,000 images are needed for each episode of *The Simpsons.*

Suddenly, it seemed, every family was rushing home to do the same. Together with *Married...With Children,* which follows *The Simpsons,* this pair of foul families jumped into the top 20 in the Nielsen ratings, a first for the Fox network. Within two months, the one-hour block had moved into the top 15. This is an amazing feat because the Fox network reaches only four-fifths of America.

An episode of *The Cosby Show, Roseanne,* or any other typical sitcom can usually be pulled together in about six weeks (and sometimes even as few as six days). But *The Simpsons* often takes six months or longer to produce one show.

The actors get together on a Thursday to rehearse for about 45 minutes. All the writers are also there, and they take notes for changes to be made to the script on Friday. On Monday, from noon to 6 P.M., the actors meet at the recording studio for final rehearsal and taping.

Shearer said that all the writers, as well as Groening and Simon, always come to the tapings. Brooks is usually there, too. "They're definitely hands-on producers, and they have absolute quality control," Shearer said. "That's why the shows are so consistent."

Shearer called the cast "quick and loose, but always professional."

"There's no tomfoolery," he added. "Sometimes we'll ad-lib just a little something. We're all funny people. But we don't experiment or play with the script. If there are any problems, the writers and producers work it out."

Executive producers (left to right) Matt Groening, James Brooks, and Sam Simon brought the Simpson family to life.

The tape of the actors' voices is sent to Klasky-Csupo animation house in Los Angeles. There, a team of more than 50 artists are all but hidden under a pile of Simpson artwork and life-size stand-ups of TV's frantic first family. And no wonder—the artists must create about 2,000 separate drawings for each show. Only after all three executive producers have given their final OK is the whole package shipped to South Korea. In South Korea, other animators produce another 14,000 images for each Simpson episode.

More than once, the show has been delivered to Fox the Friday before airing.

Back at the sound studio, Cartwright, playing Bart, squinches her face and says with a look of total surprise, "You kissed me."

Castellaneta, playing Homer, replies, "There's nothing wrong with a father kissing his own son, I think. Now, go on boy and pay attention, because if you do, one day you may achieve what we Simpsons have dreamed about for generations; you may outsmart someone."

Meet the Simpson Family

BART

This dude is as cool as any fourth grade kid can be while still wearing short pants. We're talking about Bart, of course, who is easily the most popular character on *The Simpsons*. That's no surprise. Rowdy kids have always had a knack for pleasing TV viewers.

If Bart has a direct TV ancestor, it's got to be Dennis the Menace. Dennis was the creation of a cartoonist named Hank Ketcham. The cartoonist's real-life son was named Dennis. One day, Ketcham's wife said, "Our son, Dennis, is a menace." Suddenly, Hank Ketcham had a great idea for a comic strip. Dennis's funny adventures began appearing in the comics of newspapers in the early 1950s. By the late 1950s, Dennis was a huge hit with readers around the world. A TV version, *Dennis the Menace*, first aired in 1959 and ran until 1963.

There's a lot of Dennis the Menace in Bart Simpson. But even though Bart is a cartoon and the TV Dennis was played by a real kid, Bart somehow seems a lot more real. In school, Bart's best subjects are food fighting and getting into trouble. Once, Bart switched his name on an I.Q. test with the class genius and tattletale. The harried school principal, Mr. Skinner, happily sent Bart to The Enriched Learning Center for Gifted Children. But Bart wasn't gone for long. He got into trouble at the school for gifted children, too, and he came back.

MATT GROENING

TM © Twentieth Century Fox Film Corp., 1990

Bart Simpson, the obnoxious ten-year-old son.

10

Bart takes the I.Q. exam in the episode "Bart the Genius."

That wasn't the only time Mr. Skinner tried to avoid Bart's pranks. The principal once sent Bart to France as an exchange student. "Normally, a student is selected on the basis of academic excellence or intelligence. But in Bart's case, I'm prepared to make a big exception."

While Marge goes upstairs to talk to Bart about France, Homer and Mr. Skinner keep talking about Bart. "He makes me crazy 12 months a year. At least you get the summer off," says Homer to the principal.

Marge also loses patience with Bart, but not for long. "My special little guy," she calls him.

Bart talks back to all the grown-ups in his life. This shows that he has some kind of problem with authority figures. In fact, Bart is full of little jokes and snappy comebacks. Lots of hit TV shows have used sassy, quick-witted kids for humor. On *Welcome Back, Kotter*, the high school students often used sarcastic remarks that were a lot like some of the lines Bart comes up with.

Bart cruises around on his skateboard, wearing his favorite red baseball cap and getting in the way of all the people on the sidewalk. This spike-haired rascal is always ready for action, and the action usually involves getting into mischief. Sometimes, he'll sneak into movies and make gross noises. Or he might make prank telephone calls. He's every bit the little terror that Dennis the Menace used to be.

If Bart has a direct TV ancestor, it's got to be Dennis the Menace.

Jay North played Dennis on Dennis the Menace.

Ronnie Howard as Opie on The Andy Griffith Show.

Bart would never admit it, but he looks up to Homer.

Bart may not like to admit it, but he can be a nice guy, too. He once stood up against the school bully because the bully was picking on Lisa. Bart wound up rolling home in a garbage can. "I paid the inevitable price for helping out my kid sister," he cried. But after getting some advice from Homer ("Fight dirty"), Bart returns and wages war on the bully. Plenty of other TV kids have had to deal with bullies, too: from Beaver (Jerry Mathers) on Leave It to Beaver to Opie (Ronnie Howard) on The Andy Griffith Show.

When at home, Bart will play Scrabble (if he can cheat) and video games against his dad (as long as he's winning). But most of all, he loves to hang upside down from the end of the couch and watch the cartoon Itchy and Scratchy (a violent version of Tom and Jerry) on The Krusty the Clown Show. Every kid needs a hero, and Krusty is Bart's hero. Bart is the proud owner of a Krusty blanket, lamp shade, lunch box, photograph (personally autographed by Krusty), and a talking clown doll. His regular breakfast food is Frosty Krusty Flakes. Bart's love for Krusty is very much like how Dennis the Menace felt about his hero, Cowboy Bob.

Bart's strong point isn't neatness. This cool dude hardly ever picks up his toys.

Bart would never admit it, but he looks up to Homer. In fact, he loves his whole family. But like a lot of kids, he's quick to add, "Don't make me say it." Aw, don't be afraid to say it.

HOMER

MATT GROENING

TM © Twentieth Century Fox Film Corp., 1990

Homer Simpson, the father of the Simpson family.

Homer is like a lot of dads around the world. He has the same problems, hopes, and values as any other dad. Try as he might, this father doesn't always know best. Dads have provided plenty of laughs in lots of sitcoms through the years. Homer has to be one of the funniest. Earlier TV dads, like Ward Cleaver on *Leave It to Beaver* and Jim Anderson on *Father Knows Best,* were smart, successful guys who knew how to listen to their kids. And they had good answers for their kids' questions and problems. These dads hardly ever got mad at their children.

Homer Simpson makes a lot of mistakes, but at least he's not afraid to admit it. "Gee, I'm sorry," Homer will say all too often. There was the time he got Marge a bowling ball for her birthday, even though she doesn't bowl. It was better than the gifts he had bought her before: a tackle box and a Connie Chung calendar. Homer was really disappointed when Marge decided to use the ball for herself instead of letting him have it. After all, he loves to bowl. Homer is quite different from Ward Cleaver, who liked to buy *his* wife beautiful pearls or flowers.

Homer is especially close to Bart. They like playing catch with one another in the backyard: Homer pitches and Bart catches. And after Homer learned how to beat Bart at video games, he liked playing video games with him, too. But Homer often loses his temper with his son and is likely to chase Bart to his room shouting, "Hey! Come back here, you little…."

Homer isn't the perfect kind of dad you would see on *Leave It to Beaver* (top) or *Father Knows Best* (center). But as a husband, Homer is very much like Ralph Kramden in *The Honeymooners* (bottom).

Sometimes Homer doesn't know quite how to react to Lisa, and he often resorts to bouncing her on his knee just like he did when she was a baby. This doesn't work as well now that Lisa is older. But with baby Maggie, Homer can be downright tender.

The Simpsons are a family of noisy eaters, but Homer is the loudest by far. Other TV dads have loved food, too. Ward Cleaver and Jim Anderson would come to the dinner table neatly dressed in suit coats and ties. But Homer gobbles his grub while parked in front of the TV. Even worse, he has a habit of belching in public—annoying Marge, sometimes embarrassing Lisa (but sometimes she laughs, too), and making Bart proud to be a Simpson. Homer also bets on sporting events like football games, which makes Marge angry, too. One time, he even sneaked Bart's Walkman radio into church to hear the game.

Homer is a little chunky with a round middle, and that bothers him. He checks the scale all the time. But at least he doesn't have to spend time combing his hair, because he only has two strands.

Homer works as a safety inspector at the Springfield Nuclear Power Plant. He'd love to make more money, as long as it doesn't cut into his donut breaks. He tries hard to get in good with Mr. Burns, his boss. But he's only had one bit of praise in ten years, and that was about his wife's gelatin desserts.

Homer's on-the-job difficulties are a lot like the problems Ralph Kramden had on *The Honeymooners*. Ralph worked as a bus driver. He would be completely worn out by the time he got home from work. More than anything, Ralph wanted to be a big-shot with a fancy office. But try as he might, Ralph just couldn't quite pull it off. Another famous TV dad, Archie Bunker of *All in the Family*, sweated every day on a loading dock. Archie had nothing but bad things to say about his bosses. Al Bundy, the father on *Married… With Children*, can't stand his job as a shoe salesman. So Homer Simpson is just the latest in a long line of TV fathers who get laughs with their woeful tales of work.

Every so often Homer gets to thinking about his place in life, and it depresses him. When this happens, he'll watch a lot of television. He has remarked that he can find the answers to life's problems on TV.

MARGE

Marge seems to really want a *Leave It to Beaver* home. But in the Simpson household? No way, man. And that can cause problems in the family. Of course, the Cleaver household has always been a pretty high goal to shoot for.

No matter how hard it is to have a perfect household, Marge is always trying. For starters, she always goes to church. She has a tough time getting Lisa and Bart to go to Sunday school. It's even tougher to push Homer to go to church. She'd like her family to go to more events like the opera or the ballet. But they like watching TV more.

Marge is devoted to Homer, but she gets angry with some of his crude habits. And she really blows her top when he calls her sisters, Patty and Selma, "the gruesome twosome."

Earlier sitcom moms, like June Cleaver and Donna Stone (of *The Donna Reed Show*), usually looked terrific, if not downright beautiful. Marge is a glamour girl, herself. She takes particular pride in her big blue beehive, the tallest hairdo in Springfield. Her soaring pile of hair is held together with one bobby pin.

Marge is a mother who wants the best for her family; she'd like the perfect all-American home. She seems to really want a *Leave It to Beaver* home. But in the wacky Simpson household? No way, man. And that can cause problems in the family. Of course, the Cleaver household has always been a pretty high goal to shoot for.

No matter how hard it is to have a perfect household, Marge is always trying. She'd like her family to go to more cultural events like the opera or the ballet. But they much prefer watching TV.

MATT GROENING

Marge Simpson, the Simpson matriarch.

Marge seems to really want a *Leave It to Beaver* home.

LISA

Lisa Simpson, the sax-playing older daughter.

She's three years younger than Bart, but some people might guess that she's older. And sometimes, she acts like she's Bart's mother. Lisa always lets Bart know what she thinks of his obnoxious behavior. "I don't care what anyone else says…you're a dimwit," she'll say.

In the land of TV sitcoms, little sisters seem to exist just to give older brothers somebody to tease or make fun of. In the '50s and '60s on shows like *Father Knows Best*, the teasing was pretty mild. It usually revolved around the girl's worries about a new party dress or a boy at school. But *The Simpsons* seems to take a lot of its inspiration from the brother and sister on *Married…With Children*. There, Kelly and Bud show no mercy with each other.

The Simpsons has turned the fighting between brother and sister into a fine art. Bart calls Lisa a "sniveling toad" and "an egg-sucker." But she calmly waits for her chance. There was the time Bart needed Lisa's help to prove that Krusty the Clown didn't rob a store. Bart was forced to admit, "You're smarter than me." Lisa lives for those times. She often sides with her brother when it's cool. But she turns on him when he's about to get caught.

Lisa has her quirks, too. She can play some mean blues on that baritone saxophone of hers. She complains about playing ordinary music at a school recital. Instead, she likes to play with her pal Bleeding Gums Murphy, an old musician. That promotes harmony. Because of her music, Lisa is very different from the usually dull kid sisters of other TV sitcoms.

Like the rest of the Simpson family, Lisa likes to watch TV. Krusty the Clown makes her laugh, but she likes *The Happy Little Elves* more. She also helps her mom around the house and with Maggie. In school, she doesn't get in trouble and is a fine student.

MAGGIE

MATT GROENING

TM © Twentieth Century Fox Film Corp., 1990

Maggie Simpson, the baby of the family.

Suddenly, babies are hot. Hit movies like *Three Men and a Baby* and *Look Who's Talking* found big laughs by showcasing infants. Maggie, the youngest member of the Simpson family, gets plenty of laughs, too. When Bart was in France as an exchange student, baby Maggie almost said her first word. But so far, she hasn't. That's fine, because she has no problem getting her ideas across. When she sucks really fast on her pacifier, she's scared. And Marge and Homer know she's happy when she sucks slowly.

You might think that Maggie is just the latest in a long line of TV sitcom babies, but that's not the case. In fact, there have been very few. One of the very first was Little Ricky, the TV son of Lucy and Ricky Ricardo. They were the leading characters of *I Love Lucy*, the most popular sitcom of all time. Lucille Ball and Desi Arnaz, who were married in real life, starred in the show. Little Ricky was introduced to audiences in 1953. At first, the baby was played by two sets of twins. Later, a child actor named Keith Thibodeaux took over the role.

Maggie Simpson might be the most popular baby of the 1990s. But Maggie will have to beat out Michelle, the little charmer who co-stars on TV's *Full House*. People howl with laughter when little Michelle comes out with lines like, "Cool, man!"

Maggie doesn't say anything to anyone, but that doesn't stop her from being funny. She has a hard time walking and trips a lot over her long sleep-suit. She was supposed to grow into it. She hasn't yet. Crawling is still her fastest way to get around.

The Roots of
The Simpsons

Beaver and Wally were the perfect kids in the perfect family in the popular sitcom *Leave It to Beaver*.

In the 1950s, TV painted a pretty rosy picture of American family life.

The Simpsons may be a cartoon, but it appeals to adults as much as to children. The origins of this newest hot sitcom go all the way back to the 1950s.

In the 1950s, TV painted a pretty rosy picture of American family life. Many of the most popular shows on the air were comedies. Nearly all of these comedies showed happy, "perfect" families. Family life had its little ups and downs, but no one seemed to have problems that were really serious. Most important of all, the mothers and fathers in these TV shows were understanding, caring, and very wise.

Leave It to Beaver was broadcast from 1957–63. It was probably the most popular of all of the "happy family" sitcoms. Ward and June Cleaver lived with their sons, Wally and Theodore (who was called "Beaver"), in a big house in a comfortable suburb. Ward was an accountant and June was a homemaker.

Ward and June were a loving couple who hardly ever got angry with each other. Instead of being glued to a TV set like Homer and Marge Simpson, Ward and June just liked to relax and talk with each other. They also got along wonderfully with their kids. No matter how serious Wally's or Beaver's problems at school or with their friends were to the boys, Ward and June were always willing to listen.

Things were much the same on other shows, too. *Father Knows Best* (1954–62) starred Robert Young as Jim Anderson, a guy who was a lot like Ward Cleaver.

Other early sitcoms made the mother the star of the show. Movie actress Donna Reed had a big hit with *The Donna Reed Show*, which was broadcast from 1958–66. Reed played Donna Stone, a beautiful, loving supermom.

But not every early TV sitcom was sweet and silly. There were a few that featured characters who didn't live in fancy houses or have jobs that they loved. These shows are the distant cousins of the kind of humor that is on *The Simpsons*. One of the first of the more "real" sitcoms was *The Life of Riley*, which began way back in 1949. Jackie Gleason played Chester A. Riley, a blue collar worker at an aircraft company. The first version of *The Life of Riley* lasted only until 1950. But in 1953, the show came back with William Bendix in the starring role.

Jackie Gleason, meanwhile, had become the star of his own TV show. *The Honeymooners* looked at the lives of two married couples in New York City. Gleason starred as Ralph Kramden, an overweight, loudmouthed bus driver. Kramden wanted to get rich so he could get himself and his wife, Alice, out of their grimy, tiny apartment. The Kramden's neighbors were the Nortons.

What really made *The Honeymooners* different from earlier sitcoms was how Ralph got along with his wife, Alice. It wasn't always sweet and lovey-dovey like on other shows. In fact, Ralph and Alice often shouted at each other. Alice's favorite trick was to make a crack about Ralph's weight. This would cause Ralph to shake his fist and yell, "Bang, zoom! To the moon, Alice!"

"But no matter how much [Ralph] would threaten, everyone knew he would never hurt Alice," recalled Audrey Meadows, who played Alice. "He really loved her. Besides, Alice always got the last word in."

Another of TV's great success stories was directly inspired by *The Honeymooners*. *The Flintstones* was an animated prime-time half-hour show that first aired in 1960. Like Ralph and Alice Kramden, Fred Flintstone and his wife Wilma were a working-class couple. They had their fair share of arguments—mainly about Fred's plans to get rich in a hurry. The gimmick, of course, was that the show was set in the Stone Age. And the show was animated, a first for prime-time TV.

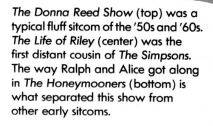

The Donna Reed Show (top) was a typical fluff sitcom of the '50s and '60s. *The Life of Riley* (center) was the first distant cousin of *The Simpsons*. The way Ralph and Alice got along in *The Honeymooners* (bottom) is what separated this show from other early sitcoms.

The Flintstones (above) was TV's first animated prime-time hit. The Jetsons (right) was directly inspired by The Flintstones.

The Simpsons follows in a long line of shows that started back in the late 1940s and early 1950s.

The Flintstones directly inspired another cartoon show, *The Jetsons*. The setting of this popular show was the distant future. The stories revolved around George Jetson, who was overworked, and his sitcom-style wife and kids. *The Jetsons* was shown in prime time during 1962 and 1963.

Many of the things that would later become part of *The Simpsons* were already in place by the mid-1960s. As a source of humor, sitcom producers depended on family situations, the worker trying to get ahead, and the difficulties of being a loving parent or mate. And prime-time animation had also been done successfully. But the time still wasn't right for anything as bold as *The Simpsons*. It took a brave TV producer named Norman Lear to lead the way.

On January 12, 1971, Lear's *All in the Family* aired for the first time. TV viewers were amused and even shocked. It was a new type of comedy that changed prime-time television forever. Archie Bunker, played by Carroll O'Connor, was like Homer Simpson in some ways. Archie Bunker was a crude, uneducated bigmouth. Other members of the family included his "dingbat" wife Edith, grown daughter Gloria, and Gloria's husband Mike. *All in the*

Family was different from dozens of other sitcoms because of the way it showed Archie's stupidity and prejudices.

All in the Family led to many new TV sitcoms. *Maude* and *The Jeffersons* were direct spinoffs of *All in the Family*. These shows and later ones like *Soap, Good Times,* and *Kate & Allie* brought a new feeling of everyday life to sitcoms. The problems of the characters weren't always silly or easily solved. Sometimes, there was no solution at all to a problem—at least not in the time given for one episode. TV viewers watched black families, families headed by divorced women, more than one family living in one house, and other sorts of situations that showed the many types of families found in everyday life.

Married...With Children is a lot like The Simpsons even though it is not a cartoon.

One of the smash hits of TV today is *Roseanne*. The comedy stars Roseanne Barr and John Goodman as a working-class couple, Roseanne and Dan Connor. People who haven't seen a sitcom since *Leave It to Beaver* or *The Donna Reed Show* would be very surprised by *Roseanne*. The Connors love each other and have a good marriage. But they're also overweight, sloppy in the way they dress, and kind of pushy, too.

The characters of Roseanne and Dan Connor owe a big debt to Ralph and Alice Kramden. "No question, it all began with *The Honeymooners*," agreed Laurie Metcalf, who plays Roseanne's sister, Jackie. "I'm not sure that *The Simpsons* is really an animated version of…*The Honeymooners,* but there's definitely a connection."

The connection between *The Simpsons* and *Roseanne* is mainly in the sharpness of much of the humor. Another very popular show, *Married…With Children,* is even more like *The Simpsons*. Although *Married…With Children* is not a cartoon, it's really more like a cartoon than a regular sitcom. Ed O'Neill and Katey Sagal star as Al and Peg Bundy, a married couple whose life is one, big, comic misery. Al hates his job as a shoe salesman. Peg can't stand Al and is fed up with her two kids.

The husband and wife on Roseanne have much in common with Ralph and Alice of The Honeymooners.

So, *The Simpsons* follows in a long line of shows that started back in the late 1940s and early 1950s with *The Life of Riley* and *The Honeymooners*. Now, let's look at the stories that make *The Simpsons* hot and in step with the 1990s.

The Simpson family plays a game in the episode "Bart the Genius."

"Bart the Genius"

This episode epitomizes the Simpson family at its best: belly-laugh humor with some biting and serious meanings. Here, school I.Q. tests are questioned. And so are parents who make accomplishments a condition for love.

The show begins with the family playing a game to help Bart get ready for the next day's I.Q. test. But Bart cheats on his I.Q. test, is hailed as a genius, and is sent to The Enriched Learning Center for Gifted Children. Suddenly, Marge and Homer shower Bart with praise and affection.

But the genius in the Simpson family is Lisa. Yet, Marge and Homer have no idea. They're too busy being nice to Bart and trying to be cultured by doing things like going to the opera.

For Steven Herbert, a television writer at the *Los Angeles Times*, "Bart looked so uncomfortable in the school for gifted children, it would have to make any viewer that relates to Bart uncomfortable. And that's a turnoff."

But Matt Roush, TV critic at *USA Today* disagreed. "Most any school kid can relate to joining a new class, and feeling out of place. That's where so much of the humor lies. But there's also a real message for adults in this episode."

"Homer's Odyssey"

Sometimes good can come out of what seems bad. That's the message you might get from an episode of *Father Knows Best*.

Bart's class goes on a field trip to the Springfield Nuclear Power Plant. When Homer shows off to the class, he

"Most any school kid can relate to joining a new class.... That's where so much of the humor lies."

causes an accident and gets fired. A saddened Homer writes a note saying goodbye. As he gets ready to dive into the river, the Simpson family shows up, yelling, "Don't do it!"

The family nearly gets hit by a car while saving Homer. Homer then saves his family by pushing them out of the way just in time. "Now, I have a purpose," says Homer. "I will not rest 'til this street gets a stop sign."

The values we see in this episode are surprisingly close to *Father Knows Best* or other TV sitcoms of the '50s and '60s. In those old sitcoms, the family always pulled together in times of crisis. The Simpson family, even Bart, helps Dad.

On the surface, it sounds like the writers of *The Simpsons* borrowed a script from some TV sitcom of the 1950s. But it works here because there's still lots of the usual crazy Simpson fun.

"Moaning Lisa"

Children worry about more things than parents can sometimes guess.

At age seven, most little girls are pretty carefree. But not Lisa. She's heading down into a blue mood. "I'm just wondering, what's the point? Would it make any difference if I never existed?" she asks her father. Of course, Homer can hardly answer such heavy questions, but he tries.

It's a problem any father can understand: what to do when his "little girl" begins to turn into a lady. The same old answers don't work anymore.

The values we see in "Homer's Odyssey" are surprisingly close to *Father Knows Best* or other TV sitcoms of the '50s and '60s.

Marge drags the family to the opera Carmen in "Bart the Genius."

MATT GROENING

TM © Twentieth Century Fox Film Corp., 1990

The Simpson family brings dessert to the company picnic in "There's No Disgrace Like Home."

"There's No Disgrace Like Home" is "a perfect example of Simpson humor at its best."

This episode is especially touching and helpful. In today's difficult world, some people think that more and more kids seem to be sad and blue. Someone lecturing about depression would never work as well for children as watching Lisa deal with it.

"There's No Disgrace Like Home."

"This show gets to the heart of the family as few sitcoms have," said Roush. "It's all a love/hate relationship."

"The truth is, we're the worst family in town," says a dejected Homer.

Homer is determined to make his family "normal." He makes the "supreme sacrifice" of selling the TV to pay for a visit to Dr. Marvin Monroe.

The family participates in "aversion parity" therapy, which uses up all of Springfield's electricity.

"It's a perfect example of Simpson humor at its best," said Roush. "The adults are laughing at what's being said, and the kids laugh at the slapstick, seeing Marge's blue hair sticking out all over and Bart's shocking expressions. It works because it's truthful."

"Bart the General"

Father doesn't always know best.

Terrorized by Nelson, the school bully, a teary-eyed Bart turns to his parents for help. Homer tells him it's OK for Bart to even the odds a little.

Finally, Grandpa Simpson takes Bart to see Herman, a crazed military surplus store clerk. With the help of Herman, Grandpa Simpson, and the other school kids, Bart wages war on Nelson the bully. The slapping scene in the movie *Patton* is wonderfully mocked. But the combat training scenes drag on too long, repeating one another.

This episode is one of the best because both parents and kids can see themselves in it. At one time or another, almost every kid—even the coolest of dudes—gets bullied. And Bart plays out their fantasy by waging war on the bad guy. It's a problem for parents, too. Most fathers don't offer the advice Homer does. But deep down inside, most dads would love to.

"Call of the Simpsons"

Not every episode can be a gem of deep insight into the world. "This episode is more like *The Flintstones* than the more thought-provoking *Simpsons*," Roush commented.

The show starts off well. It explores the roots of envy. Bart eyes the neighbor's fancy riding mower. But Homer tells him, "Just be happy with what you've got. Don't try to keep up with the Flanderses."

But when Mr. Flanders drives up in a fancy new RV, Homer forgets his own advice. Homer immediately takes the family shopping for an RV. The funniest moments come when a sneaky RV salesman sells Homer the only thing he can afford; an old, broken-down camper.

The camping trip starts off fun. But the show just turns into silliness after the camper falls off a cliff. It's great fun for children viewers. But much of the episode doesn't have any adult appeal.

"This [episode] is larger than life," said Roush. "The Simpsons are at their best when they manage to replicate real life."

"The Telltale Head"

"How important is it to be popular?" Bart asks his father.

"I'm glad you asked, son," replies Homer. "Being popular is the most important thing in the world."

Both parents and kids can see themselves in "Bart the General."

To a ten-year-old child, popularity is an important matter. Bart has a problem with popularity. Should he do a bad thing to win the praise of some of the bad kids in school? Armed with his father's advice, Bart takes the head off the statue of the town's honored founder—Jebediah Springfield. Then the trouble begins.

This show is successful in several ways. It offers an important message for kids: Do what you think is right, not what you think your friends want. It also does a good job of showing all the people in the town in several scenes. In most cartoons, only a few characters are shown closely at one time.

Bart, as usual, starts all the trouble.

"Life on the Fast Lane"

Roush called this show "as funny as any episode of any sitcom can get." It is a very well done episode.

Staying true to the one you love is the serious theme. But, of course, *The Simpsons* explores the topic with wit.

For Marge's 34th birthday, Homer gives her a bowling ball. She's never bowled before, but she decides to use the gift that Homer really wants for himself. A bowler named Jacques makes friends with her.

Homer feels that Marge is slipping away from him. So he compliments her on her excellent peanut butter and jelly sandwiches.

"You can see how much Marge means to Homer," said Roush. "He's absolutely crushed. It's really quite touching in a way."

"Homer's Night Out"

The message in this show is that everyone is a real person and no one should be treated as just an object. The Simpson family may wind up teaching the world a thing or two in the 1990s.

Bart, as usual, starts all the trouble. He uses his new spy camera to snap a picture of Homer dancing at a party.

As you might expect, Bart takes the picture to school. Soon it's all over town. But Homer's fame means big trouble at home. Marge is angry and ashamed of Homer. For penance, he must apologize. But that's easier said than done.

"The Crepes of Wrath"

Bart gets in trouble again at school. And the principal convinces Homer and Marge to send Bart to France as an exchange student. Bart's gone, and the Simpsons host Adil Hoxha. Adil is a courteous, affectionate Albanian boy, and Homer likes him instantly.

But looks can fool people. And there's another side to Adil. Meanwhile, Bart, over in France, is worked to the bone by two French wine makers.

This show is funny in its spoof of spy stories. And Bart learns an important lesson: He loves his family more than he thought.

"Krusty Gets Busted"

It's a clever whodunit, *Simpsons*-style. It also makes fun of all those movies where the faith of a little boy saves a fallen hero. In this case, the fallen hero is Krusty the Clown.

One day, Krusty is arrested for robbing the local Kwik-E Mart. Bart feels horrible. Bart is sure Krusty was framed, and he asks Lisa to help him.

"It's an all too familiar story today," said Steven Herbert. "It's the story of a fallen idol. You'll notice that Krusty was virtually deemed guilty by the town even before the trial began." But Krusty has a friend on his side—none other than Bart Simpson.

"Some Enchanted Evening"

Steven Herbert called this episode "the most interesting and innovative."

Homer treats Marge to a night on the town. Meanwhile, Ms. Botz babysits the children. Bart and Lisa watch the TV show *America's Most Armed and Dangerous* and find out that "Ms. Botz" is actually Lucille Botzcowski, the notorious Babysitter Bandit.

"They successfully spoof one of the Fox network programs, *America's Most Wanted*. And they even come up with a better name," Herbert added.

Roush said, "This story is a quintessential Simpson adventure. TV reality coming to life in their own home."

"Krusty Gets Busted" deals with a familiar theme—the fallen hero.

27

The craze for The Simpsons is everywhere, even making it to the covers of national magazines like entertainment weekly.

A Craze
in the Making

"From the beginning, we were just a little ship. And we don't want to become a big luxury cruise liner."

It's radical, dude! No one would have believed it. A TV network, usually begging for publicity for its shows, has actually cut back on publicity.

The Fox network, worried about overhype, has started to just say no to any publicity about *The Simpsons*. The network has turned down interview requests (up to 100 during some weeks) with any of the main actors or executive producers.

"From the beginning, we were just a little ship," said Harry Shearer to Steve Dale. "And we don't want to become a big luxury cruise liner. But now, the little boat is being whipped around by a delightful, but strong, cyclone of outside pressure. The challenge is to insulate the show from those big winds."

Too much publicity could spoil the show. Matt Roush, TV critic at *USA Today*, explained, "Fox doesn't want another *ALF*. There were *ALF* parties on college campuses. And the young kids were absolutely devoted viewers, buying *ALF* dolls, T-shirts, and all the rest. Then, the show fell into the toilet. It sank from the top 10 to the top 40 [in the Nielsen ratings]. Of course, *ALF* was never quite as sophisticated as *The Simpsons*."

Some of the typical Simpson products—buttons, posters, and T-shirts—available at many J.C. Penney stores.

TM © Twentieth Century Fox Film Corp., 1990

TM © Twentieth Century Fox Film Corp., 1990

Although some smaller stores are having trouble stocking Simpson merchandise, the J.C. Penney chain is having no problem at all.

But is *The Simpsons* show as harmless as *ALF*? Could watching *The Simpsons* really be bad for kids? "There are worse models in life, and even on television, than Bart Simpson," said Paul Hirsch, a sociologist and professor at the Kellogg Graduate School of Management at Northwestern University, Evanston, Illinois.

Hirsch explained the appeal of *The Simpsons*. He said the show reveals some of today's attitudes. For example, said Hirsch, "The yuppies as a group can relate to the Simpson family's 'I don't give a [darn] about the other guy' attitude, because they don't either. It's clearly a depressing statement about our society."

DON'T HAVE A COW, MAN!

RADICAL DUDE!

Everyone has their favorite character. Lecy Goranson, 15, who plays Becky on *Roseanne,* is a big fan of Lisa Simpson. "She's me in real life. I still fight with my older brother, just like she does with Bart. And like my character on *Roseanne,* she's kind of like the straight kid."

Roush pinpointed another part of the show's attraction. He called the Simpson family a blast of fresh, but sour, air. "They're as sour as the Bundys [from *Married…With Children*] and as likable as the Huxtables [from *The Cosby Show*]. You can't beat that mix for the '90s. This show's in for a long run."

In each episode, there is usually something that hits home. You may see a part of yourself that you can laugh at. Or, there may be an example of *The Simpsons* making light of everyday, difficult problems. In today's world of TV violence, Simpson comedy is bold and heartening. And that appeals to everyone.

But most Simpson fans don't study the show, they just laugh. "It's one of my all-time favorite programs," Goranson cheered.

Licensed Simpson products include water bottles (left), bumper stickers (center), and hats (lower right).

TM © Twentieth Century Fox Film Corp., 1990

There are about 70 licensed Simpson products. Bart posters (below) undoubtedly decorate the walls of many kids' rooms. The Simpson beach towel (right) is a big seller in Los Angeles.

TM © Twentieth Century Fox Film Corp., 1990

The show's popularity fueled a bottomless appetite for Simpson products.

The shows's popularity fueled a bottomless appetite for Simpson products. There was a public demand, practically an outcry, for Simpson products. This was very different from the usual merchandising seen for karate-chopping turtles or movies like *Batman*. Now, there are some 70 licensed Simpson products. Have sales slowed? No way, man. And Twentieth Century Fox is laughing all the way to the bank. The company gets a cut based on the sale of licensed products.

The list of products includes T-shirts, Maggie note pads, beach towels, water bottles, buttons, and posters. There are also life jackets (including a mini-Maggie jacket for toddlers) and a Bart talking doll (sorry, it doesn't belch).

Eric Lieberson is the vice-president of Jazz'd, an up-scale chain of T-shirt stores in Southern California. His store in Westwood Village, Los Angeles, was the first to sell Simpson products exclusively. "Our biggest seller is the Simpson family beach towel," he said.

"Unlike the [Teenage Mutant Ninja] Turtle merchandise, which was purchased mostly by kids, the adults are also buying Simpson products for themselves. And they have more money to spend. It's an incredible phenomenon. Batman merchandise set store records, yet this is ten times better."

Stores continue to steadily sell Teenage Mutant Ninja Turtle merchandise. But Lieberson says that he can't keep up with the demand for Simpson products.

Frank Damico is the manager of Fun, Inc., located in Livonia, Michigan. Fun, Inc., is a subsidiary of Gags and Games, which has five stores around Detroit. Gags and Games also operates 22 stores that open exclusively during the Halloween season. "I'm expecting our best Halloween ever," said Damico.

Especially popular are Simpson buttons with sayings from the show's characters.

STAY OUTTA MY ROOM, MAN!

GO FOR IT, DUDE !!

NO WAY MAN!

WATCH IT DUDE

BART SIMPSON

TM © Twentieth Century Fox Film Corp., 1990

An array of Simpson goods at a J.C. Penney store.

Charles Giovenco, manager of Fantasy Headquarters in Chicago, agreed. "Dick Tracy will be hot with adults, and the kids will be getting into turtle shells, but the Simpsons appeal to entire families."

Damico, Giovenco, and Robert Proce, owner of Razzle-Dazzle Costumes in Oak Park, Illinois, all agreed that last year's top Halloween costumes were Freddy Krueger from the *Nightmare on Elm Street* movies and Batman. After those two came Elvira of the TV show *Movie Macabre*. They predict things will get more competitive this season in the kids' department. The Teenage Mutant Ninja Turtles will run neck and neck with Bart and Lisa Simpson.

Bart and Lisa Simpson will run neck and neck with the Teenage Mutant Ninja Turtles for kids' Halloween costumes this year.

When you're driving down the road, you'll see Simpson characters on car windows. The messages can be nice ("Have you hugged your kid today?" or "Peace, dude"), typical Bartisms ("Outta my way, man"), or takeoffs of movies ("Bartman on board").

Adults can simply put on a fedora and wear a trench coat for the Dick Tracy look. Other hot sellers will include the ever popular Freddy and Elvira as well as masks of Tracy's arch enemies, Prune Face and Flattop. But Homer and Marge Simpson are expected to be the first couple of Halloween. "They'll put Ron and Nancy [Reagan], George and Barbara [Bush], and Frankenstein and his bride to shame," Proce added.

At the same time, the number of non-licensed products is huge. At a White Sox game at Comiskey Park in Chicago, the vendors who were selling Simpson T-shirts and baseball caps were making out like bandits. Buyers stood in long lines for the Simpson gear. The fans even seemed annoyed by the vendors who tried to sell White Sox stuff. But, hey, even the White Sox vendors were proudly wearing Bartman shirts.

Twentieth Century Fox Film Corp. is taking any sales of non-licensed Simpson goods very seriously. The company is suing several distributors of non-licensed Simpson products. Twentieth Century Fox is cracking down on unauthorized items to protect itself as well as the program's image. Some of the more extreme examples of unauthorized goods are in poor taste.

Clothing is always a popular item to use for licensed products. Typical examples include underwear (below) and T-shirts (right).

TM © Twentieth Century Fox Film Corp., 1990

But some stores say they're forced to use fake merchandise. "We've had several T-shirts on request for months at a time without a response [from the licensee]," said one store. "Meanwhile, our customers are demanding them." Many small businesses have had the same difficulty getting Simpson products to sell. But big stores, like J.C. Penney, have no problem filling a thousand of their stores with Simpson products.

No matter how hard Fox tries to control Simpson publicity and product sales, the popularity of *The Simpsons* keeps soaring. Examples of the show's popularity are everywhere. This mutant Walton family stole the show at the Second Animation Celebration in New York City. The Simpsons appear on a TV commercial for Butterfinger candy bars. (Bart says, "Nobody better lay a finger on my Butterfinger.") And they've been the theme of many college dorm parties. Cool, huh?

Examples of the show's popularity are everywhere.

The Groening of America

The Simpson family—Lisa, Homer, Bart, Marge, and Maggie (left to right)—is the demented creation of Matt Groening.

Everyone knows the no-good kid in your neighborhood. He's the one who tears the wings and maybe a leg or two off a grasshopper. Then he lets the maimed insect go to get by as best it can.

In a way, Matt Groening, the devilishly clever mind behind *The Simpsons*, does the same thing to his hapless, quarreling TV family. No, Groening doesn't cruelly take the Simpsons apart piece by piece. (But there's no doubt that Homer Simpson is tempted every so often to rip Bart apart for his latest bratty prank.) Groening does take away the brains and patience the Simpson family needs to survive in Springfield.

As much as the Simpsons want to be "normal" and "popular," they just can't get it right. In one episode, Marge is surprised that the families the Simpsons spy on "actually enjoy talking to each other." And in the same episode, Homer recalls, "My mom once said something that really stuck with me. She said, 'Homer, you're a big disappointment.' And God bless her soul, she was really on to something."

Groening may be pretty nasty to his characters, but he's really a friendly guy who laughs easily. And Groening has good reason to be happy these days. His animated sitcom and his comic strip featuring Binky the Rabbit have made him one of the hottest cartoonists today.

Groening never planned to be a cartoonist. He really wanted to be a writer.

Groening—husky and bearded—never planned to be a cartoonist. He was the third of five children and grew up in Portland, Oregon. Groening's father made advertising films and did some cartooning. And Groening's dad was named Homer. All the other Simpson characters, except Marge and Bart (which is a play on the word "brat"), are also named after members of Groening's family. But the real-life family members think more, are nicer, and act less rashly than the family members on The Simpsons.

Groening did his share of cartoon drawing when he was a boy. And he was often rewarded for it with a trip to the principal's office—a place Bart knows so well. But drawing cartoons was just a way to goof off and have a few laughs with his friends. Groening really wanted to be a writer. He showed some childhood promise. In 1962, he won a short story writing contest in the magazine Jack and Jill.

Groening attended The Evergreen State College in Olympia, Washington. Evergreen didn't give grades and had no required classes. That suited Groening perfectly. He had plenty of time to work on the student newspaper. Groening graduated in 1977. He left the Pacific Northwest and headed for Los Angeles to become a writer.

But things didn't happen quite as he planned. Instead of writing newspaper or magazine articles, he worked as a chauffeur and "biographer" for an 88-year-old director of really bad movies. Groening drove the man around and listened to his stories. In the evening, he typed up notes about the stories. This was not a very good start for a hopeful writer.

The rest of Groening's life wasn't so good either. He lived in a small apartment. The guy downstairs liked to play loud rock 'n' roll in the middle of the night. At first, Groening tried to get back at him by blasting reggae music. He finally got his point across by dropping a cinder block on the floor. That knocked out his neighbor's ceiling light.

But this small victory didn't make up for his other disappointments. Groening couldn't stand the Los Angeles smog and unattractive vistas. And his lack of professional progress was a big letdown.

TM © Twentieth Century Fox Film Corp., 1990

Groening named the Simpson family members (except Bart and Marge) after his own family members. Homer was his father's name.

The misadventures of Binky and his friends led to one major result: *The Simpsons.*

So, for relief, he decided to send a message to his friends back home. It wasn't a boring letter telling about his unhappiness. Instead, it was a comic book about life in Los Angeles. The comic strip starred a somewhat bitter and simply drawn rabbit named Binky. A rabbit was the only figure Groening was able to draw. The rabbit's name, he told *Los Angeles* magazine in 1985, was the "stupidest" he could think of.

Soon the strip was a small underground success in Los Angeles. Groening was now making 500 copies instead of 20. In 1980, the strip started to appear in the Los Angeles *Reader*, a weekly paper where Groening worked as an editor/delivery man.

But many readers were annoyed by Binky's habit of yelling about hip slang like "boogie" and "ambience." To stir more interest in the strip, Groening changed the rabbit from a grump to a victim. "The second my characters began to be tortured and alienated, the popularity began," he told *Newsweek* in 1987. "The more I tortured them, the more readers loved me."

The adventures of Binky—and his girlfriend Sheba and one-eared son Bongo—struck a chord. With his buck teeth and bulging eyes, Binky looks kind of like a raggedy Trix cereal rabbit. The strip isn't the best-drawn in the world. That's OK—the words are the real attraction. Groening often crams every spare bit of space around his drawings with text. As a matter of fact, Groening sometimes calls himself a writer who happens to be a cartoonist.

In 1987, Groening married Deborah Caplan. She had joined the *Reader* advertising staff about the same time he had started there. By their wedding day, they had quit the *Reader* to spend all their time working on the comic strip. The strip was getting the attention of more and more newspapers. It was also causing a mini-industry of T-shirts, mugs, and other goods. Now ten years old, the comic strip runs in more than 200 newspapers. And many of the strips have been collected in books.

The misadventures of Binky and his friends led to one major result: *The Simpsons.* They share many of the same views and ideas as the characters portrayed in the comic strip. There may be rabbits in one and people in the other, but the characters are directly linked.

TM © Twentieth Century Fox Film Corp., 1990

Groening, shown here with cutouts of Bart, Homer, and Lisa, uses *The Simpsons* to showcase his own humorous view of today's modern family.

Groening's career as a cartoonist had a humble start: the comic strip starring Binky the Rabbit.

In the comic strip, bullies beat up helpless children, lovers hurt each other, and brothers and sisters fight. In *The Simpsons,* bullies beat up Bart, Homer neglects Marge, and Bart and Lisa quarrel. The comic strip asks the question, "Why is TV so cool?" It answers, "It allows several people who hate each other to sit peacefully together in the same room for years on end without murdering each other." In *The Simpsons,* the only time the family doesn't argue is when the TV has their attention.

This may seem a bleak view of things, but it is Groening's view. And much of America is laughing at the wit and humor Groening shows through this modern family. Not bad for a guy who never planned to be a cartoonist.

Of course, Groening can't do *The Simpsons* alone. He gets lots of help from two people who know a lot about TV and movies: James L. Brooks and Sam Simon.

James Brooks is an executive producer for the show. The area around his fireplace at home is filled with awards, including three Oscars and nine Emmys. His TV credits include *Room 222, The Mary Tyler Moore Show, Rhoda, Taxi,* and *Lou Grant.*

Groening gets lots of help from two people who know a lot about TV and movies: James L. Brooks and Sam Simon.

Brooks (left) and Simon (right) pose with cutouts of three Simpson characters. *The Simpsons* is another in a long line of hit TV shows that these two have been involved with.

TM © Twentieth Century Fox Film Corp., 1990

The idea for *The Simpsons* got started on *The Tracey Ullman Show*.

Brooks wrote the screenplay and co-produced the movie *Starting Over* in 1979. In 1983, he picked up an Oscar for *Terms of Endearment*. He also wrote, directed, and produced *Broadcast News* in 1987. His movie production company produced *Say Anything…* and *War of the Roses*. He also co-produced *Big*.

In 1987, Brooks returned to TV as executive producer of *The Tracey Ullman Show*. And that's where the idea for *The Simpsons* got started.

Sam Simon is a writer for *The Simpsons* and is also an executive producer for the show. He has won Emmys as the writer and producer of *Taxi, It's Garry Shandling's Show*, and *The Tracey Ullman Show*.

Like Groening, Simon also began his career as a cartoonist. He wrote and designed characters for several Saturday morning cartoons. In 1981, he left the world of Saturday morning cartoons. Today, he also sometimes directs *The Tracey Ullman Show* or an episode of *The Simpsons*.

Together, these three creative people have come up with one of the hottest shows on TV.

The Voices Behind the Characters

The animated characters on the screen are only a part of the charm of *The Simpsons*. Homer, Bart, and all the others need actors to bring them to life.

Dan Castellaneta has a long acting history that includes stints with Second City in Chicago and *The Tracey Ullman Show*. He plays Homer Simpson, as well as several other characters, on *The Simpsons*.

Nancy Cartwright

Nancy Cartwright plays the obnoxious Bart. Cartoons were her specialty long before *The Simpsons*. Her voice has been featured in a seemingly endless array of Saturday morning cartoons, including *Galaxy High, Fantastic Max, Richie Rich, Snorks, Pound Puppies, My Little Pony,* and *Glo-Friends*.

Tracey Ullman added Cartwright to the cast of her show in 1987.

As Bart, Cartwright gets as much mail as all the other cast members combined. "The piles of mail are bigger than she is," said Harry Shearer to Steve Dale, a columnist with *Inside Chicago*. "She is more surprised than anyone that her character has become a modern day folk hero."

Dan Castellaneta

On *The Simpsons*, Castellaneta usually plays several characters in each episode. But his biggest role is as Homer. Among other roles, he has played Krusty the Clown, Barney, and one of the French hosts to Bart.

Castellaneta is a native of the Chicago area. He has been acting since he was six years old. His first voice character was an impersonation of old-time movie star Edward G. Robinson.

He made it to the stage, working in classics like *A Midsummer Night's Dream* and *The Taming of the Shrew*. He also performed in the Chicago area children's program *Beyond the Magic Door*.

From 1983 to 1987, Castellaneta performed at Chicago's Second City. While there, he learned about improvisation and sliding in and out of characters. These lessons came in handy for *The Simpsons*.

Tracey Ullman saw Castellaneta performing at Second City when she was in Chicago filming *Vise Versa*. Castellaneta turned down an offer to be in the *Nothing in Common* TV series to work with Ullman. Ullman's flexible structure and the chance to play all kinds of characters interested him more.

Castellaneta has also done voice work in more than 100 commercials.

Harry Shearer's voice is perfectly suited for playing many of Springfield's oddballs.

Julie Kavner

Julie Kavner, who plays Marge, is probably the cast member most familiar to television audiences. After all, in *Rhoda* who can forget Rhoda's sister, Brenda Morgenstern? Kavner played Brenda from 1971 to 1978. She won the Emmy for Best Supporting Actress in a Comedy Series in 1978. Kavner has been on Tracey Ullman's show since Ullman's series started on Fox.

Kavner has also worked with Woody Allen. She's appeared in several of his films, including *Hannah and Her Sisters, New York Stories,* and *Crimes and Misdemeanors*. She also has a part in *Awakenings,* a movie also starring Robin Williams and Robert De Niro.

In *The Simpsons,* Kavner also plays Marge's sisters, Patty and Selma.

Yeardley Smith

Yeardley Smith plays the character of Lisa on *The Simpsons*. Smith is a very experienced actress with a wide range of roles in movies and TV. She's appeared in such

Julie Kavner—best known for her role as Rhoda's sister on *Rhoda*—supplies the voice of Marge Simpson.

feature films as *She-Devil, Silence Like Glass, Heaven Help Us,* and *Maximum Overdrive.*

On TV, she co-starred in *Mom's on Strike,* an After School Special. She has also guest starred on *Sydney, Brothers, Mama's Family, Murphy Brown,* and *The Tracey Ullman Show.*

On Broadway, Smith appeared in Tom Stoppard's play *The Real Thing.*

Harry Shearer

Harry Shearer's voice is like a rubber band. It is perfectly suited for playing many of Springfield's oddballs. He's played Herman of Herman's Military Antiques, Dr. Marvin Monroe, the local school bus driver, Mr. Burns (Homer's boss), and the flower shop owner.

Once a regular on *Saturday Night Live,* Shearer began his career as a child actor on Jack Benny's radio show. Shearer went to school at UCLA in the 1960s. While there, he was the editor of the school's humor magazine. Later, he was a founding member of the comedy troupe The Credibility Gap.

Kelsey Grammer (left) played Sideshow Bob in the "Krusty Gets Busted" episode. Albert Brooks (right)—star of the movie *Lost in America*—is just one of several actors whose voices are heard on *The Simpsons.*

Shearer appeared in the original *Leave It to Beaver* pilot as Eddie Haskell. He also appeared on *GE Theatre* and *Alfred Hitchcock Presents.* Shearer was a creator and a star of the feature film *This Is Spinal Tap.* He has appeared in *The Right Stuff* and several other films. He also had his own HBO special, *HBO Comedy Hour Live: The Magic of Live.*

Right now, Shearer's *Le Show* radio program is syndicated around the country. He is a regular contributing editor for *Spy* magazine and a columnist for the *Los Angeles Times Sunday Magazine.*

Guest stars

One attraction of *The Simpsons* is the recognizable guest voices that appear now and then. When you first hear a guest voice, it always brings a jolt of surprise.

In the first season of *The Simpsons*, actor/comedian Albert Brooks appeared as the slimy RV salesman. The unmistakable voice of Penny Marshall (costar of *Laverne* and Shirley; director of *Big*) can be heard as Lucille Botzcowski, the Babysitter Bandit. Kelsey Grammer, who plays Dr. Frasier Crane on *Cheers*, had a big role as Sideshow Bob in the "Krusty Gets Busted" episode. And Mrs. Crabapple, Bart's "annoying" teacher, is played by Marcia Wallace. From 1972 to 1978, Wallace played Carol the receptionist on *The Bob Newhart Show*.

Harvey Fierstein (left) will supply a guest voice during the 1990–91 season, and Whoopi Goldberg (right) has offered to do the voice of Maggie if Maggie ever talks.

We can look forward to more of the same kind of interesting guest voices in this upcoming season. Harvey Fierstein (*Torch Song Trilogy*) and television veteran Tom Poston will both make guest appearances. Performers ranging from Roseanne Barr to Michael Jackson are also willing to lend their voices to TV's new first family. And Whoopi Goldberg has said that she wants to play Maggie if Maggie ever speaks. For now, Matt Groening provides the sucking sounds for Maggie.

I. Multiple Choice

1. Before she became the voice of Bart, Nancy Cartwright was a voice for characters on which cartoon show(s)?

   A. Fantastic Max
   B. Glo-Friends
   C. Pound Puppies
   D. Richie Rich
   E. All of the above

2. At first, Matt Groening really wanted to be a:

   A. Nuclear safety inspector
   B. Doctor
   C. Bus driver
   D. Writer
   E. None of the above

3. One of Lisa's favorite things to do is:

   A. Play blues saxophone with Bleeding Gums Murphy.
   B. Pull the wings off insects.
   C. Eat pizza.
   D. Wash her feet in the kitchen sink.

4. Once, Homer celebrated Marge's birthday by giving her:

   A. A diamond ring
   B. A Connie Chung calendar
   C. A life-size poster of Elvis Presley
   D. A package of blue dye for her hair

5. Who gets shot out of a cannon on Krusty the Clown's TV show?

   A. Homer Simpson
   B. Mrs. Crabapple
   C. Tracey Ullman
   D. Sideshow Bob

6. Bart Simpson is very much like what other famous TV kid?

A. Beaver Cleaver
B. Marcia Brady
C. Dennis the Menace
D. Kevin Arnold

7. Some of the Simpson products you can buy today are:

A. Beach towels
B. Bumper stickers
C. T-shirts
D. Buttons
E. All of the above

8. Harry Shearer plays lots of characters on *The Simpsons*. Which character does he *not* play?

A. Dr. Marvin Monroe
B. Mr. Burns, Homer's boss
C. Herman of Herman's Military Antiques
D. Mr. Skinner, the school principal

II. Fill in the Blank

1. The sucking sounds Maggie makes are supplied by _____.

2. The name of the town the Simpson family lives in is _____.

3. "The Gruesome Twosome" is Homer's name for _____.

4. The Simpson Christmas special was called _____.

5. In 1962, Matt Groening won a short story writing contest in the magazine _____.

6. _____ is famous for saying "Don't have a cow, man."

7. The founder of the town of Springfield was _____.

8. The name of the opera that Marge drags the family to was _____.

9. _____ has volunteered to play the voice of baby Maggie, if Maggie ever speaks.

10. To make one episode of *The Simpsons* may take as many as _____ drawings.

III. True or False

1. Homer was named after Matt Groening's dad.

   True   False

2. *The Simpsons* is the first hit animated show to appear on prime-time TV since *The Jetsons* came out 28 years ago.

   True   False

3. Homer works as a janitor in an office building.

   True   False

4. James L. Brooks, who produces *The Simpsons,* also produced other hit TV shows like *Room 222* and *Lou Grant*.

   True   False

5. For Marge's 34th birthday, Bart got her a book of poems.

   True   False

6. When the Simpson family goes to the company picnic, they bring along gelatin desserts.

   True   False

7. An episode of *The Simpsons* can be produced in as short a time as a week.

   True   False

Answers to section I: 1:E; 2:D; 3:A; 4:B; 5:D; 6:C; 7:E; 8:D **Answers to section II:** 1: Matt Groening; 2: Springfield; 3: Marge's sisters, Patty and Selma; 4: "The Simpsons Roasting on an Open Fire"; 5: *Jack and Jill;* 6: Bart Simpson; 7: Jebediah Springfield; 8: *Carmen;* 9: Whoopi Goldberg; 10: 14,000. **Answers to section III:** 1:True; 2:True; 3:False, Homer works at a nuclear power plant; 4:True; 5:False, Bart got her French perfume; 6:True; 7:False, One episode takes about six months.